TOOLS OF THE TRADE

Anna,
So good to see you
and have the thread over
the years...
Enjoy!
love,
Lesley x

TOOLS OF THE TRADE
POEMS FOR NEW DOCTORS

Edited by
Dr Lesley Morrison
Dr John Gillies
Revd Ali Newell
Samuel Tongue

Scottish **Poetry** Library

Polygon

This edition published in 2019 by The Scottish Poetry Library
5 Crichton's Close, Edinburgh EH8 8DT and
Polygon, an imprint of Birlinn Ltd
West Newington House, 10 Newington Road,
Edinburgh EH9 1QS

Reprinted 2020

9 8 7 6 5 4 3 2

First published in 2014 by the Scottish Poetry Library

www.scottishpoetrylibrary.org.uk
www.polygonbooks.co.uk

ISBN 978 1 84697 488 5

Typeset in Verdigris MVB by Polygon, Edinburgh
Printed and bound by Gutenberg Press, Malta

The publishers are grateful for all the donations
towards the cost of this anthology

CONTENTS

II. LOOKING AFTER OTHERS

III. BEGINNINGS

IV. BEING WITH ILLNESS

V. ENDINGS

Many congratulations on graduating as a doctor. We wish you all the very best for a satisfying, fulfilling and enjoyable career.

Tools of the Trade is offered as a friend and companion when you need support, comfort or encouragement. We hope you find in it poems which speak to your experience, resonate with how you feel and make what the poet Mary Oliver called 'this one, wild and precious life' seem better.

Being a doctor is a privilege; patients will share stories with you which no one else may ever have heard. The art of listening, *really* listening, is a very special one and one which teaches you about your patients and about yourself. In order to look after patients, we need to look after, and be kind to, ourselves as well.

The book is divided into five sections: *looking after yourself, looking after others, beginnings, being with illness* and *endings*. The criteria for choosing the poems were that they were short, accessible and spoke in some way to the experience of being a junior doctor; there are poems about compassion, tiredness, worry, and longing for the outdoors. We know that poetry may not initially appeal to everyone but we challenge you to find at least one poem in *Tools* which speaks directly to you and your experience.

We are grateful to the Medical and Dental Defence Union of Scotland (MDDUS) and the Royal College of General Practitioners Scotland (RCGP) for their generous support of this third edition, and to the Scottish Poetry Library, especially Samuel Tongue, for his commitment and dedication to the project.

So . . . carry the poems with you and enjoy them. Speak them out loud and use them as tools to connect with your patients, your colleagues and yourself.

Dr Lesley Morrison MRCGP;
Dr John Gillies, OBE, FRSE,
FRCGP, FRCP Edin; and
Revd Ali Newell

Poems for doctors. An odd concept? Poems for doctors funded by a medical defence organisation. Even odder. Where's the evidence and data? Where's the fit with the scientific training?

What these poems show – and your own professional practice will increasingly demonstrate – is that not everything is a matter of hard-edged scientific evidence or financial calculation. It's not all a matter of intellect, observation, diagnostic or manual skills. Imagination, empathy and insight into your own position can be just as important – and sometimes even more so when it comes to building trust and rapport, to communicating the best and worst of news and guiding and sharing decision-making.

That's where this little book comes in. You will know where to turn for training and data to build knowledge, but help to stimulate the reflective, self-aware practice that is essential in modern medicine, and the resources which help you to care for yourself – and so continue to care properly for your patients – may be harder to find. Your partners and colleagues will provide this insight and support to you, just as you will provide it to them.

In a different way, so do these poems. They capture moments of celebration, uncertainty, and helplessness for doctor and patient alike – and those points of 'terrible beauty' which engage a wide range of emotions, simultaneously, sometimes in the oddest combinations, and so provide the richest reflections.

MDDUS is delighted to provide support for a new edition of *Tools of the Trade: Poems for New Doctors*, a resource for you to draw on in both the quiet and thoughtful moments of your career and perhaps at its most challenging times as well.

Chris Kenny , CEO
The Medical and Dental
Defence Union of Scotland

INTRODUCTION

There's a great deal of science in medicine – science allied with a healthy dose of human kindness. But much of the work we do as doctors could just as profitably be described as an art: knowing not just what to do, but when, why and how it should be done. Too little has been written about the art of finding ways, as someone who cares for others, of caring for yourself.

This book will help. John Keats, who trained as a doctor, counselled that the best poetry should strike you as 'a wording of your own highest thoughts'. Emily Dickinson wrote that poets should tell the truth, but 'tell it slant'. Whether you hated poetry at school or keep volumes by your bedside you'll find something here to appreciate, now and in the years to come: poems that will grant new, slanting perspectives on familiar clinical thoughts. From Kathleen Jamie's revelation of the beauty and power of ultrasound, to Cynthia Huntington's account of being on the other side of the clinic desk; from Dannie Abse's revelations with a stethoscope, to Bob Hicock's elegiac account of dementia, there are wonders in these pages – fifty or so reminders that for all the science in medicine, through all its challenges and rewards, to practise it well remains an art.

Gavin Francis, FRCGP, FRCPE
gavinfrancis.com

I. LOOKING AFTER YOURSELF

New doctors will be empowered by poems
in the pockets of their metaphorical white coats.
There at the ready:
on early, sweaty, scratchy, ward rounds
to deploy while waiting patiently for the consultant's
    late appraisal;
give filing, phlebotomy and form-filling an edge
    and depth;
sweeten tea-breaks as if with juxtaposed Jaffa Cakes
to answer that persistent bleep – while sneaking a pee,
to travel the manic crash and flat-lined emptiness of
    cardiac arrest
thole the inevitability of the inevitable;
to pace with careful cadence;
stop and breathe usefully
arrive ready not to recite by rote;
to be alone with on the boisterous bus home
to txt anxious Mums and Dads – 'Are you remembering
    to feed yourself?'
'yes. lol. Smiley-face – perhaps a frog?'
to place strategically on the cup-ringed cabinet – first
    night on-call,
thrust under the sun-torn pillow on the morning
    following the first night on-call
find undisturbed, but at a different verse, following the

jumpy party, following the first night on-call
to steal insights into the science of nurses' smiles
to prepare for change.
To take a full history, examine closely and reach a working
    diagnosis: 'You are a human being.'
    'The stars sing as whitely as the mountains.'
To investigate with prudence.
To reconsider the prognosis in the light of better-quality
    information.
To appreciate; pass on; ponder challenge, relinquish,
allow, accept
be accosted by dignity.
To forgive and free.

Màrtainn Mac an t-Saoir
Martin MacIntyre

THE DOOR

Go and open the door.
       Maybe outside there's
       a tree, or a wood,
       a garden,
       or a magic city.

Go and open the door.
       Maybe a dog's rummaging.
       Maybe you'll see a face,
or an eye,
or the picture
       of a picture.

Go and open the door.
       If there's a fog
       it will clear.

Go and open the door.
       Even if there's only
       the darkness ticking,
       even if there's only
       the hollow wind,

even if
            nothing
                is there,
go and open the door.

At least
there'll be
a draught.

Miroslav Holub
translated by Ian Milner

THE GUEST HOUSE

This being human is a guest house.
Every morning a new arrival.

A joy, a depression, a meanness,
some momentary awareness comes
as an unexpected visitor.

Welcome and entertain them all!
Even if they're a crowd of sorrows,
who violently sweep your house
empty of its furniture,
still, treat each guest honorably.
He may be clearing you out
for some new delight.

The dark thought, the shame, the malice,
meet them at the door laughing,
and invite them in.

Be grateful for whoever comes,
because each has been sent
as a guide from beyond.

Jelaluddin Rumi
translated by Coleman Barks

THE PEACE OF WILD THINGS

When despair for the world grows in me
and I wake in the night at the least sound
in fear of what my life and my children's lives may be,
I go and lie down where the wood drake
rests in his beauty on the water, and the great heron feeds.
I come into the peace of wild things
who do not tax their lives with forethought
of grief. I come into the presence of still water.
And I feel above me the day-blind stars
waiting with their light. For a time
I rest in the grace of the world, and am free.

Wendell Berry

GIFT

A day so happy.
Fog lifted early, I worked in the garden.
Hummingbirds were stopping over honeysuckle flowers.
There was no thing on earth I wanted to possess.
I knew no one worth my envying him.
Whatever evil I had suffered, I forgot.
To think that once I was the same man did not embarrass me.
In my body I felt no pain.
When straightening up, I saw the blue sea and sails.

Czesław Miłosz

from 'DISENCHANTMENTS'

Mineral loneliness. The hour of stone.
A boat cut loose. Not much to steer it with.
Grey branches hanging over Acheron.

Look to the living, love them, and hold on.

Douglas Dunn

BEANNACHT / BLESSING

for Josie, my mother

On the day when
the weight deadens
on your shoulders
and you stumble,
may the clay dance
to balance you.

And when your eyes
freeze behind
the grey window
and the ghost of loss
gets in to you,
may a flock of colours,
indigo, red, green
and azure blue,
come to awaken in you
a meadow of delight.

When the canvas frays
in the currach of thought
and a stain of ocean
blackens beneath you,

may there come across the waters
a path of yellow moonlight
to bring you safely home.

May the nourishment of the earth be yours,
may the clarity of light be yours,
may the fluency of the ocean be yours,
may the protection of the ancestors be yours.

And so may a slow
wind work these words
of love around you,
an invisible cloak
to mind your life.

John O'Donohue

CATCHING UP ON SLEEP

I go to bed early
to catch up on my sleep
                      but my sleep
is a slippery customer
it bobs and weaves
                and leaves
me exhausted. It
side steps my clumsy tackles
with ease. Bed
raggled I drag
myself to my knees.

The sheep are countless
I pretend to snore
yearn for chloroform
or a sock on the jaw
body sweats heart beats
there is Panic in the Sheets
until
as dawn slopes up the stairs
to set me free
unawares
sleep catches up on me.

                    Roger McGough

POEM FOR A HOSPITAL WALL

Love has been loitering
down this corridor
has been seen
chatting up out-patients
spinning the wheels of wheelchairs
fluttering the pulse of the night nurse
appearing, disguised, as a bunch of grapes and a smile
hiding in dreams
handing out wings in orthopedics
adding a wee drappie
aphrodisiaccy
to every prescription.
No heart is ever by-passed by Love.

Love has been loitering down this corridor
is highly infectious
mind how you go. If you smile
you might catch it.

Diana Hendry

TALKING TO THE FAMILY

My white coat waits in the corner
like a father.
I will wear it to meet the sister
in her white shoes and organza dress
in the live of winter,

the milkless husband
holding the baby.

I will tell them.

They will put it together
and take it apart.
Their voices will buzz.
The cut ends of their nerves
will curl.

I will take off the coat,
drive home,
and replace the light bulb in the hall.

John Stone

To every thing there is a season, and a time to every
purpose under the heaven:
A time to be born, and a time to die; a time to plant, and
a time to pluck up that which is planted;
A time to kill, and a time to heal; a time to break down,
and a time to build up;
A time to weep, and a time to laugh; a time to mourn, and
a time to dance;
A time to cast away stones, and a time to gather stones
together; a time to embrace, and a time to refrain
from embracing;
A time to get, and a time to lose; a time to keep, and a time
to cast away;
A time to rend, and a time to sew; a time to keep silence,
and a time to speak;
A time to love, and a time to hate; a time of war, and a
time of peace.

PSALM EIGHTY-EIGHT BLUES

Lord, when I'm speechless
when something – not just sorrow
but under that – a dull, numb, nameless dreich
about the heart I hardly seem to have,
when this afflicts me,
when hope's been cancelled,
when the pilot light of me's put out,
when every reflex and response
has been extinguished,

send word, snowdrop, child, light.

Diana Hendry

WINTER WOOD

So I have put away the books
and I watch the last apples fall
from the frosty trees

and I have seen also
acorns stretching red shoots
into the hard soil

and the white bark of the birches
was more to me than all the pages

and what I read there
bared my heart to the winter sun
and opened my brain to the wind

and suddenly
suddenly in the midst of that winter wood
I knew I had always been there

before the books
as after the books
a winter wood

and my heart bare
and my brain open to the wind.

                    Kenneth White

II. LOOKING AFTER OTHERS

THE PRECIOUS 10 MINUTES

The GP stands at the door of his room,
shakes my hand, asks me how I am.
I always smile and say fine, except for . . .
this niggling problem
or I'm just here for a checkup
or a repeat prescription
or something.

He listens.
He's a cautious man, gets me tested
just in case: 'Let's be sure.'

He sounds me out about an ongoing condition:
if I can live with it
he can live with it.
'As long as you can do the things
you want to do.'
He knows I'm a worrier.

I don't feel rushed.
It's a conversation.
It all seems as it should be.

Hamish Whyte

JACKSON SPANDER

Acute and chronic bronchitis

He hadn't the wits to show me signs
Like his friend had done
To convince me he was crazy enough to be committed,
Just for the winter.

He hadn't the courage to say he was famished
That his bedsore was oozing stinking pus
That he didn't have the strength to ride the boxcar
To Pensacola this year
That he thought he was afraid of dying
On a park bench.

He didn't even know that he was asking me to take
    care of him:
'Hell, Doc, I was takin care of myself
Before your Daddy had fuzz on his chin!'
And when he laughed he hacked his bloody phlegm
Through a toothless, smelly grin
And filled his paper cup.

But he spent that winter on my ward
In the V.A. hospital.

                        K.D. Beernink

BEDSIDE TEACHING

No one steps forward
We look at the floor, he picks
Me. What can you feel?

Tentatively, I
Press down on her abdomen
The loose skin, lost curves

Hard and craggy ruins
Beneath. My heart sinks into
Her diseased belly

No time left to think
What is your diagnosis?
Don't make me say it

Everybody knows
What is your diagnosis?
Not in front of her

He watches me burn
I won't say Cancer. Not here
Think hard. It could be . . .

Eyebrows raised, eyes turn
I need a technical term
It escapes like a

Mouse dropped by a cat
It could be a malignancy.
And I am a fool

Mitotic disease
He corrects. We must employ
Some euphemisms.

Rachel Bingham

MAMMOGRAM

'They're benign,' the radiologist says,
pointing to specks on the x-ray
that look like dust motes
stopped cold in their dance.
His words take my spine like flame.
I suddenly love
the radiologist, the nurse, my paper gown,
the vapid print on the dressing room wall.
I pull on my radiant clothes.
I step out into the Hanging Gardens, the Taj Mahal,
the Niagara Falls of the parking lot.

                    Jo McDougall

A BRIEF FORMAT TO BE USED WHEN
CONSULTING WITH PATIENTS

The patient will talk.

The doctor will talk.

The doctor will listen while
the patient is talking.

The patient will listen while
the doctor is talking.

The patient will think that the doctor
knows what the doctor is talking about.

The doctor will think that the patient
knows what the patient is talking about.

The patient will think that the doctor
knows what the patient is talking about.

The doctor will think that the patient
knows what the doctor is talking about.

The doctor will be sure.
The patient will be sure.

The patient will be sure.
The doctor will be sure.

Shouldn't hurt a bit, should it?

Glenn Colquhoun

A MEDICAL EDUCATION

for Dr Peter Rothwell

In obstetrics I learnt that a woman opens swiftly like an
    elevator door.
The body wriggles free like people leaving an office on a
    wet afternoon.

In medicine I learnt that the body is the inside of a watch.
We hunch carefully over tables with blunt instruments.

In paediatrics I learnt that the body is a bird.
I leave small pieces of bread in fine trails.

In geriatrics I saw that the neck becomes the shape of an
    apple core.
In intensive care I discovered that the body is a number.

The sick sweat like schoolboys studying maths before
    a test.
In orthopaedics I found that the body can be broken.

Bones make angles under skin as though they were part of
    a collapsed tent.
In anaesthetics I saw people hang on narrow stalks like
    ripe apples.

But in the delivery suite I learnt to swear.

                              Glenn Colquhoun

THE STETHOSCOPE

       Through it,
over young women's abdomens tense,
I have heard the sound of creation
and, in a dead man's chest, the silence
  before creation began.

       Should I
pray therefore? Hold this instrument in awe
and aloft a procession of banners?
Hang this thing in the interior
  of a cold, mushroom-dark church?

       Should I
kneel before it, chant an apophthegm
from a small text? Mimic priest or rabbi,
the swaying noises of religious men?
  Never! Yet I could praise it.

       I should
by doing so celebrate my own ears,
by praising them praise speech at midnight
when men become philosophers;
  laughter of the sane and insane;

                night cries
of injured creatures, wide-eyed or blind;
moonlight sonatas on a needle;
lovers with doves in their throats; the wind
    travelling from where it began.

Dannie Abse

from PLAYING GOD

10. A note of warning to patients when all else fails

Sometimes the needle is too blunt.
The stethoscope is too quiet.
The scalpel will not cut.
The scissors chew like old men's gums.

Sometimes the book has not been written.
The pill cannot be swallowed.
The crutches are too short.
The x-rays hide like dirty windows.

Sometimes the thermometer will not rise.
The plaster will not stick.
The stitches cannot hold.
The heart conducts a normal ECG.

Then I have to ask you what to do

Which is what you might
have wanted all along.

Glenn Colquhoun

THESE ARE THE HANDS

These are the hands
That touch us first
Feel your head
Find the pulse
And make your bed.

These are the hands
That tap your back
Test the skin
Hold your arm
Wheel the bin
Change the bulb
Fix the drip
Pour the jug
Replace your hip.

These are the hands
That fill the bath
Mop the floor
Flick the switch
Soothe the sore
Burn the swabs
Give us a jab
Throw out sharps
Design the lab.

And these are the hands
That stop the leaks
Empty the pan
Wipe the pipes
Carry the can
Clamp the veins
Make the cast
Log the dose
And touch us last.

Michael Rosen

POSTSCRIPT

And some time make the time to drive out west
Into County Clare, along the Flaggy Shore,
In September or October, when the wind
And the light are working off each other
So that the ocean on one side is wild
With foam and glitter, and inland among stones
The surface of a slate-grey lake is lit
By the earthed lightning of a flock of swans,
Their feathers roughed and ruffling, white on white,
Their fully grown headstrong-looking heads
Tucked or cresting or busy underwater.
Useless to think you'll park and capture it
More thoroughly. You are neither here nor there,
A hurry through which known and strange things pass
As big soft buffetings come at the car sideways
And catch the heart off guard and blow it open.

Seamus Heaney

III. BEGINNINGS

OPENING

A gestation reaches its timely conclusion
Her muscled hammock softens, slackens
I am with her wet slit, hands quiet ready

A head down pressure, spine to belly
Her womb bow taut as a new balloon
I hear heart beat code, pains come, go

A tuft of hair appears, recedes to tease
Her skin peels over a spongy first frown
I map read headland suture, fontanelle

A flicker of eyelids, phantom of a new
Her hands clutch knees, chin tucks in
I prop her heel on my hip, bear down

A nose tips. Bloodline, too early to know
Her guttural sounds, deep, old as Eve
I breathe in rhythm between her pushes

A fold of ear unfurls as lips pucker apart
Her fingers stretch over, stroke baby hair
I loosen cord. A rough touch can mutilate

A breath held moment. Bruise blue runs to red
Her opening forgotten already starts to close.

Helen Catherine Sheppard

from ULTRASOUND

for Duncan

1. Ultrasound

Oh whistle and I'll come to ye,
my lad, my wee shilpit ghost
summonsed from tomorrow.

Second sight,
a seer's mothy flicker,
an inner sprite:

this is what I see
with eyes closed;
a keek-aboot among secrets.

If Pandora
could have scanned
her dark box,

and kept it locked –
this ghoul's skull, punched eyes
is tiny Hope's,

hauled silver-quick
in a net of sound,
then, for pity's sake, lowered.

Kathleen Jamie

TWENTY-EIGHT WEEKS

We nearly missed her.
This little storm of life,
could have blown by
before we weathered her.
But here she is: sturdy,
definite, pointing her finger
for this and this and more
and more and more.

Lesley Glaister

TEDDY

for a child with leukaemia

Teddy was not well.
Teddy had been feeling sick.
Teddy had to go to hospital.
Teddy was told that he had too much blood.
Teddy did not miss his friends.
Teddy knew the thermometer was not sharp.
Teddy was not scared of needles.
Teddy said the medicine would make him better.
Teddy closed his eyes at night.
Teddy ate his vegetables.

Teddy's small girl lay in the corner of his bed.
She was not so sure.
Her eyes were made from round buttons.
The fluff on the top of her head was worn
as though it had been chewed.

Glenn Colquhoun

ADAM, THERE ARE ANIMALS

There is a small fox
slipping through the fabric of morning,
still coated in a layer of grey dusk

and carefully placing his paws
between what's left of night
in the garden.

There is a monkey,
a stained toy, in your hand
when you arrive at the hospital,

which none of the fussing people
had noticed
and you had clung to.

There are wild-eyed soldiers' horses,
charging at us from the jigsaw pieces
in the waiting room

where we try to sleep
on the table and chairs
and pretend we're not waiting.

There are several pigeons
on the window ledge, shuffling about
before the steel chimneys and pinking sky

and a seagull's bark
in the deflated quiet
just after you die.

There is an overfed cat
in the arms of a nurse who smokes
by the automatic doors.

and there are baby rabbits
eating the grass verges
of the hospital car park.

There is our dog
at the door, confused
when we get home without you.

And on the kitchen table we sit at, dazed
and not quite real, with cups of tea to hold on to,
there is a small plastic horse.

Chloe Morrish

MY PAPA'S WALTZ

The whiskey on your breath
Could make a small boy dizzy;
But I hung on like death:
Such waltzing was not easy.

We romped until the pans
Slid from the kitchen shelf;
My mother's countenance
Could not unfrown itself.

The hand that held my wrist
Was battered on one knuckle;
At every step you missed
My right ear scraped a buckle.

You beat time on my head
With a palm caked hard by dirt,
Then waltzed me off to bed
Still clinging to your shirt.

Theodore Roethke

CHILDREN'S WARD WEEK TWO

While she's in theatre
he walks the corridors,

rides a lift with five pink balloons
and a new Dad wearing the smile
he once had,

joins the dressing gowns at the front door,
challenging fate with cigarettes,

passes a woman carrying someone's effects
in a black bin bag,

stops at a place he's long ignored
with a banner embroidered
Your name is written on the palms of my hands

and a book of pleas
too hard to read

and stays
to struggle with the litany
make her name his prayer.

Iora Dawes

IV. BEING WITH ILLNESS

RECOVERY ROOM

The noise in the recovery room
Was half footfall and half hum

Like a well-mannered gallery
Of pictures that I could not see.

And then a name disrupted it:
The hated name of childhood: Pat,

A name I had not answered to
For fifty years and would not now.

Another voice began to talk:
Pat. And still I did not speak.

My husband waited in my room
And in the end they sent for him,

After an hour or two of this.
I heard Patricia. And said 'Yes?'

Patricia Beer

MULTIPLE SCLEROSIS

For ten years I would not say the name.
I said: episode. Said: setback, incident,
exacerbation – anything but be specific
in the way this is specific, not a theory
or description, but a diagnosis.
I said: muscle, weakness, numbness, fatigue.
I said vertigo, neuritis, lesion, spasm.
Remission. Progression. Recurrence. Deficit.

But the name, the ugly sound of it, I refused.
There are two words. The last one means: scarring.
It means what grows hard, and cannot be repaired.
The first one means: repeating, or myriad,
consisting of many parts, increasing in number,
happening over and over, without end.

Cynthia Huntington

MYELOMA MOTHS

The moths came with a soft flutter
one night and burrowed into
the deepest recesses of cloth.

Their offspring had their fill, gnawed
the wool and cashmere mix of a coat
framed by a hanger, shaped like you.

They punched out holes, some like stars
which didn't shine, coalesced into craters.
Silver dust littered the wardrobe carpet.

They were driven out, killed off a few times,
but younger generations grew,
attacked the arms, shoulders and back

until the coat was held together by threads.
Shrunken and spineless its days were numbered,
it shed bits of blue wool like tears.

                    Karen Patricia Schofield

LUCK

Patient:

Here's a good one I saw
on an obscure cable station today.

(I think they mostly interview farmers who see aliens
land in their cornfields and housewives

inhabiting someone else's body.) So this middle-aged
man was saying how he gave up smoking last month

and now his surgeon just told him there's a lesion
in his lung and it's lucky because it's curable.

So this man (I think from Pittsburgh) says, Just like
it's lucky for those two kids pulled from

a burning building. If it's lucky, how come
they got second-degree burns? How come

they were in the building in the first place? Want to hear about real luck? he says, staring straight at the camera.

I have this itch under my arm. I'll scratch it twice in slow circles and my cancer is gone.

Marc Straus

NOW WHERE?

It wakes when I wake, walks
when I walk, turns back when I
turn back, beating me to the door.

It spoils my food and steals
my sleep, and mocks me, saying,
'Where is your God now?'

And so, like a widow, I lie down
after supper. If I lie down
or sit up it's all the same:

the days and nights bear me along.
To strangers I must seem
alive. Spring comes, summer;

cool clear weather; heat, rain . . .

Jane Kenyon

THINGS

There are worse things than having behaved foolishly
    in public.
There are worse things than these miniature betrayals,
committed or endured or suspected; there are worse
    things
than not being able to sleep for thinking about them.
It is 5 a.m. All the worse things come stalking in
and stand icily about the bed looking worse and worse
    and worse.

Fleur Adcock

IATROGENIC

You say, 'I do this to myself.' Outside,
my other patients wait. Maybe snow falls;
we're all just waiting for our deaths to come,
we're all just hoping it won't hurt too much.
You say, 'It makes it seem less lonely here.'
I study them, as if the deep red cuts
were only wounds, as if they didn't hurt
so much. The way you hold your upturned arms,
the cuts seem aimed at your unshaven face.
Outside, my other patients wait their turns.
I run gloved fingertips along their course,
as if I could touch pain itself, as if
by touching pain I might alleviate
my own despair. You say, 'It's snowing, Doc.'
The snow, instead of howling, soundlessly
comes down. I think you think it's beautiful;
I say, 'This isn't all about the snow,
is it?' The way you hold your upturned arms,
I think about embracing you, but don't.
I think, 'We do this to ourselves.' I think
the falling snow explains itself to us,
blinding, faceless, and so deeply wounding.

Rafael Campo

THE UNPROFESSIONALS

When the worst thing happens,
That uproots the future,
That you must live for every hour of your future,

They come,
Unorganised, inarticulate, unprofessional;

They come sheepishly, sit with you, holding hands,
From tea to tea, from Anadin to Valium,
Sleeping on put-you-ups, answering the phone,
Coming in shifts, spontaneously,

Talking sometimes,
About wallflowers, and fishing, and why
Dealing with Kleenex and kettles,
Doing the washing up and the shopping,

Like civilians in a shelter, under bombardment,
Holding hands and sitting it out
Through the immortality of all the seconds,
Until the blunting of time.

U.A. Fanthorpe

CT SCAN

It's an atlas of eight plates
filled with slice after slice
of inner space: the laminate
topographies laid out,
some like star maps,
organic galaxies,

some like Mercator projections
of island chains on inland seas
and none warn of dragons –
there's no dark matter
and no shadows in the water
but there is a reason

for this space-sickness
and this cold sweat. There,
on the fifth plate; on the half-
shell profile of one kidney
lies my own cultured pearl:
a perfect circle of white fire.

Rob Evans

TO MY SURGEON

No one else sees me
drowning in the white wave
sprinkled with a terrible salt

invasive lobular carcinoma
is difficult to identify

but you take one look
and I am

held
by your hand
saving my life

Valerie Gillies

H E

EYE

CHART

I scowl towards his voice. He says the map
marks how far vision goes. If I could creep

up close I'd learn the journey. His technique
restricts me to a chair so he can track

how far I travel down the chart alone
before I pause. I grope in the third line –

my limit the next shape I recognise –
then stop. No way. I still believe my eyes

can hold a solar system, catch all the lights,
deliver to the doctor alphabets

as small as atoms. But this world is smudge.
I'm huddled at the bottom of the page,

trying to hide my dark. Wherever I am,
I've bypassed every symbol I can name

and stumble at my vision's borders
where letters are illegible as stars.

Nuala Watt

TIRED BLOOD

Well, not *tired*
so much as *freighted*.
As though foreign objects
had invaded.
As though tiny offices
had dumped their metal furniture
among the glossy lozenges
and platelets –
chairs that stick together,
painful cabinets.

                              Kay Ryan

SECOND OPINION

We went to Leeds for a second opinion.
After her name was called,
I waited among the apparently well
And those with bandaged eyes and dark spectacles.

A heavy mother shuffled with bad feet
And a stick, a pad over one eye,
Leaving her children warned in their seats.
The minutes went by like a winter.

They called me in. What moment worse
Than that young doctor trying to explain?
'It's large and growing.' 'What is?' 'Malignancy.'
'Why there? She's an artist!'

He shrugged and said, 'Nobody knows.'
He warned me it might spread. 'Spread?'
My body ached to suffer like her twin
And touch the cure with lips and healing sesames.

No image, no straw to support me – nothing
To hear or see. No leaves rustling in sunlight.
Only the mind sliding against events
And the antiseptic whiff of destiny.

Professional anxiety –
His hand on my shoulder
Showing me to the door, a scent of soap,
Medical fingers, and his wedding ring.

Douglas Dunn

HEALINGS 2

At midnight the north sky is blues and greys, with a thin
    fissure of citrine
just above the horizon. It's light when you wake,
    regardless of the hour.
At 2 or 4 or 6 a.m., you breathe light into your body.

A rose, a briar rose. A wild rose and its thorned stem.
    What did Burns say?
'you seize the flo'er, the bloom is shed'.

To be healed is not to be saved from mortality, but rather,
    released back into it:
we are returned to the wild, into possibilities for ageing
    and change.

Kathleen Jamie

THE OLD LADY

Autumn, and the nights are darkening.
The old lady tells us of her past once more.
She muses on the days she spent nursing

at ten shillings a month. 'And what exams!
I could understand anything in those days.
What summers we had then, what lovely autumns.'

And so I imagine her cycling to her work
among the golden leaves, down avenues,
to hospitals which were disciplined and stark

with hard-faced matrons, doctors jovial
with an authority that was never quizzed,
while grizzled Death suckled at his phial,

and autumn glowed and died, outside the ward,
and girlishly she saw it fade in red
in sky and sheet, and evening was barred
with strange sweet clouds that hung above the bed.

Iain Crichton Smith

HIS STILLNESS

The doctor said to my father, 'You asked me
to tell you when nothing more could be done.
That's what I'm telling you now.' My father
sat quite still, as he always did,
especially not moving his eyes. I had thought
he would rave if he understood he would die,
wave his arms and cry out. He sat up,
thin, and clean, in his clean gown,
like a holy man. The doctor said,
'There are things we can do which might give you time,
but we cannot cure you.' My father said,
'Thank you.' And he sat, motionless, alone,
with the dignity of a foreign leader.
I sat beside him. This was my father.
He had known he was mortal. I had feared they would
    have to
tie him down. I had not remembered
he had always held still and kept quiet to bear things,
the liquor a way to keep still. I had not
known him. My father had dignity. At the
end of his life his life began
to wake in me.

                    Sharon Olds

NOTHING

Because she is exhausted
and confused,

and doesn't want to argue,
and can't speak,

she dreams of nothing
for a thousand years,

or what the nurses cheerfully call
a week.

Selima Hill

ALZHEIMER'S

Chairs move by themselves, and books.
Grandchildren visit, stand
new and nameless, their faces' puzzles
missing pieces. She's like a fish

in deep ocean, its body made of light.
She floats through rooms, through
my eyes, an old woman bereft
of chronicle, the parable of her life.

And though she's almost a child
there's still blood between us:
I passed through her to arrive.
So I protect her from knives,

stairs, from the street that calls
as rivers do, a summons to walk away,
to follow. And dress her,
demonstrate how buttons work,

when she sometimes looks up
and says my name, the sound arriving
like the trill of a bird so rare
it's rumored no longer to exist.

                                    Bob Hicok

WHAT THE DOCTOR SAID

He said it doesn't look good
he said it looks bad in fact real bad
he said I counted thirty-two of them on one lung before
I quit counting them
I said I'm glad I wouldn't want to know
about any more being there than that
he said are you a religious man do you kneel down
in forest groves and let yourself ask for help
when you come to a waterfall
mist blowing against your face and arms
do you stop and ask for understanding at those moments
I said not yet but I intend to start today
he said I'm real sorry he said
I wish I had some other kind of news to give you
I said Amen and he said something else
I didn't catch and not knowing what else to do
and not wanting him to have to repeat it
and me to have to fully digest it
I just looked at him
for a minute and he looked back it was then
I jumped up and shook hands with this man who'd just
given me
something no one else on earth had ever given me
I may have even thanked him habit being so strong

Raymond Carver

THE FIRST DEATH

I was surprised
how quickly
his body turned cold
so soon after
the terrifying task
listening to the emptiness with my stethoscope
 to pronounce

the first death

how wide his eyes under my penlight
unblinking
how heavy his wrist, how still

how easily tears flowed when the routine of death
the autopsy request
the certificate for the morgue
was punctuated by
a sigh
for the hole left in his family

how much his kids look like him

Andrea Wershof Schwartz

from CLEARANCES

In the last minutes he said more to her
Almost than in all their life together.
'You'll be in New Row on Monday night
And I'll come up for you and you'll be glad
When I walk in the door . . . Isn't that right?'
His head was bent down to her propped-up head.
She could not hear but we were overjoyed.
He called her good and girl. Then she was dead,
The searching for a pulsebeat was abandoned
And we all knew one thing by being there.
The space we stood around had been emptied
Into us to keep, it penetrated
Clearances that suddenly stood open.
High cries were felled and a pure change happened.

Seamus Heaney

from CUMHA CHALUIM IAIN MʜɪᴄGILL-EAIN

Tha an saoghal fhathast àlainn
ged nach eil thu ann.
Is labhar an Uibhist a' Ghàidhlig
ged tha thusa an Cnoc Hàllainn
is do bhial gun chainnt

Somhairle MacGill-Eain

from ELEGY FOR CALUM I. MacLEAN

The world is still beautiful
though you are not in it,
Gaelic is eloquent in Uist
though you are in Hallin Hill
and your mouth without speech

Sorley MacLean

TALKING TO GRIEF

Ah, grief, I should not treat you
like a homeless dog
who comes to the back door
for a crust, for a meatless bone.
I should trust you.

I should coax you
into the house and give you
your own corner,
a worn mat to lie on,
your own water dish.

You think I don't know you've been living
under my porch.
You long for your real place to be readied
before winter comes. You need
your name,
your collar and tag. You need
the right to warn off intruders,
to consider
my house your own
and me your person
and yourself
my own dog

Denise Levertov

AT EIGHTY

Push the boat out, compañeros,
push the boat out, whatever the sea.
Who says we cannot guide ourselves
through the boiling reefs, black as they are,
the enemy of us all makes sure of it!
Mariners, keep good watch always
for that last passage of blue water
we have heard of and long to reach
(no matter if we cannot, no matter!)
in our eighty-year-old timbers
leaky and patched as they are but sweet
well seasoned with the scent of woods
long perished, serviceable still
in unarrested pungency
of salt and blistering sunlight. Out,
push it all out into the unknown!
Unknown is best, it beckons best,
like distant ships in mist, or bells
clanging ruthless from stormy buoys.

Edwin Morgan

GOING WITHOUT SAYING

i.m. Joe Flynn

It is a great pity we don't know
When the dead are going to die
So that, over a last companionable
Drink, we could tell them
How much we liked them.

Happy the man who, dying, can
Place his hand on his heart and say:
'At least I didn't neglect to tell
The thrush how beautifully she sings.'

Bernard O'Donoghue

NOTES ON SOME OF THE POEMS
AND DOCTOR POETS

Dannie Abse (1923–2014) was a Welsh poet and chest consultant.

Kenneth Dale Beernink (1938–1969) was an American poet and doctor. His one collection of poems, *Ward Rounds*, was published posthumously.

Rafael Campo (b. 1964) is an American poet, essayist and doctor.

Glenn Colquhoun (b. 1964) is a New Zealand poet, children's writer and GP.

'Things' / Fleur Adcock
When the first line of this poem popped into my head it struck me as something people can identify with. I was pleased when the unnamed 'things' – our worst personal anxieties, whatever they may be – took on a life of their own. We all recognise them.

'The Unprofessionals' / Described by R.V. Bailey
U.A. Fanthorpe's poem is about what happened when our friends' son, who was at home, unwell, from university, suddenly vanished – along with the family car. The car was later found by a river, but there was never any trace of the boy. Apart from being with his parents, there was little that anyone could do. But they did what they could.

In order to write, Fanthorpe abandoned a career in education and became an NHS hospital clerk, an experience that pitchforked her into poetry. In 2002 she was awarded the Queen's Gold Medal for Poetry.

'A Brief Format . . .' / Glenn Colquhoun
I love the consultation. It is the high altar of medicine, God and priest and man all in the same place at the same time, no one knowing who is who and someone always roaming around. It strikes me how much is assumed within it and how most of the time those assumptions are accurate . . . most of the time.

'Teddy' / Glenn Colquhoun
I wrote this poem for a three-year-old patient with leukaemia. She screamed at her doctors whenever we entered her room on the ward. On Christmas Day Santa Claus gave her a water pistol. After that we were allowed in as long as we were shot one by one

without mercy. She is well now and trains dogs. Water pistols should be a mainstay of cancer treatment.

'A medical education' / Glenn Colquhoun

I wrote the poems in *Playing God* as a young doctor and so many of my experiences in medicine were experiences I was having for the first time. I felt as though I was bobbing from flowerbed to flowerbed in some huge botanical garden. I was encountering the body as a character for the first time and learning that each part carried its own personality.

from 'Playing God' / Glenn Colquhoun

There is a great deal of medicine that doctors possess not because they have been to medical school but because they have lived life. They have been sons and daughters and mothers and fathers and friends and lovers. Sometimes it is the medicine these experiences teach us that is the most powerful of all.

'To My Surgeon' / Valerie Gillies

This poem recalls what it feels like to be the patient who hears that mammogram and biopsy have missed the cancer and that it has gone undetected for a long time. I owe my life to a surgeon who was sharp-eyed and persistent enough to diagnose this particular cancer.

'Ultrasound' / Kathleen Jamie

I loved the ultrasound image of my baby. Humans are very visual, we seem to have actually to see something to believe it. Also, I was interested in the relationship between sound and image. Ultrasound was non-invasive, exciting, confirming. But the grainy grey image made the baby seem like a ghost, a wee ghoul from the future, not the past. Not a scary ghost, but one you'd feel tender towards.

'Poem for a Hospital Wall' / Diana Hendry

This poem was written when I was writer-in-residence at Dumfries & Galloway Royal Infirmary. There was an artist working there too – Rachel Mimiec – and she wrote or painted the poem on a corridor wall of the hospital. We used the passages off as line breaks!

'Psalm Eighty-Eight Blues' / Diana Hendry

In an Oxfam bookshop, I found, Peter Hately Waddell's *The Psalms: Fra Hebrew intil Scottis*. I loved them. 'Psalm Eighty-Eight Blues' was prompted by the epigraph to Psalm 88 which reads 'A cry from the heart to God, neither light nor hopeful'. I think my poem is a prayer.

'Tools of the Trade' / Martin MacIntyre

I wrote 'Tools of the Trade' in response to the announcement of the bold plan to gift a collection of poems to newly graduated doctors in Scotland; I was delighted when it was accepted for this important book. Drawing on my own medical experience and that of others, I tried to convey the power of poetry to support, inform and re-humanise and its crucial place in the survival armoury of health professionals and their patients.

'Going Without Saying' / Bernard O'Donoghue
The poem was written after the death of a friend of mine – a successful industrial chemist in his 40s with a lovely wife and three children, who committed suicide totally unexpectedly. His devastated wife was partly comforted by a letter he left, saying how much he loved and admired her.

'Jackson Spander', selected by the editors from a public call, promoted by leading medical journals, for poem submissions / Described by Dr Alex Scott-Samuel, public health physician, Liverpool
Kenneth Dale Beernink was a brilliant young doctor who tragically died of chronic myelogenous leukaemia in 1969, four years after he graduated at Stanford University. During his internship at Yale and later at Stanford he wrote a series of case study poems featuring patients of all ages and a wide range of pathologies and social circumstances. They are all highly sensitive, deeply caring and beautifully crafted.

'The Precious 10 Minutes' / Hamish Whyte

The poem is for my GP, Dr Ian Davey, who has looked after me with care and consideration since I moved to Edinburgh in 2004. Unfortunately he's now retired, but at least he'll have more time for his wonderful photographs of birds, some of which brightened up his surgery.

ACKNOWLEDGEMENTS

Our thanks are due to the following authors, publishers and estates who have generously given permission to reproduce works:

Dannie Abse, 'Stethoscope' from *New Selected Poems: 1949-2009*, by permission of Sheep Meadow Press and The Random House Archive and Library; Fleur Adcock, 'Things' from *Poems 1960–2000* (Bloodaxe Books, 2000), by permission of the publisher; Patricia Beer, 'Recovery Room' from *Autumn* (Carcanet, 1997), by permission of the publisher; Wendell Berry, 'The Peace of Wild Things' from *New Collected Poems* (Counterpoint, 2012) Copyright © 2012 by Wendell Berry, reprinted by permission of Counterpoint; Rachel Bingham, 'Bedside Teaching' from *The Annual Hippocrates Prize Anthology 2017* by permission of the author. Rafael Campo, 'Iatrogenic' from *Alternative Medicine* (Duke University Press, 2013) Copyright © by Rafael Campo. Reprinted by permission of Georges Borchardt, Inc., for the author; Raymond Carver, 'What the Doctor Said' from *All of Us* (Harvill Press, 1997), reprinted by permission of The Random House Group Limited;

Glenn Colquhoun, 'A medical education', 'A brief format to be used when consulting with patients', 'Teddy', and 'A note of warning to patients when all else fails', from *Playing God: Poems about Medicine* (Steele Roberts, 2002), by permission of the publisher; Iora Dawes, 'Children's Ward Week Two' from *The Annual Hippocrates Prize Anthology 2017*, by permission of the author; Douglas Dunn, 'Second Opinion', from *Elegies* (Faber & Faber Ltd, 1985), and 'Disenchantments', from *Dante's Drum-kit* (Faber & Faber Ltd, 1993) by permission of the publisher; Rob Evans. 'CT Scan' from *The Annual Hippocrates Prize Anthology 2017*, by permission of the author; U.A. Fanthorpe, 'The Unprofessionals' from *New and Collected Poems*, (Enitharmon Press, 2010) by permission of R.V. Bailey; Valerie Gillies, 'To My Surgeon', from *The Hand That Sees: Poems for the Quincentenary of the Royal College of Surgeons of Edinburgh* (Royal College of Surgeons of Edinburgh / Scottish Poetry Library, 2005) by permission of the author; Lesley Glaister, 'Twenty-eight Weeks', from *Visiting the Animal* (Mariscat Press, 2015), by permission of the author; W.S. Graham, from 'Private Poem to Norman MacLeod' from *New Collected Poems* (Faber & Faber, 2005), by permission of Rosalind Mudaliar, the Estate of W.S. Graham; Seamus Heaney, 'Clearances', from *The Haw Lantern* (Faber & Faber Ltd, 1997), by permission of the publisher; 'Postscript', from *Opened Ground: Selected Poems, 1966–1996* (Farrar, Straus and Giroux, 2002), by

Levertov, reprinted by permission of New Directions Publishing Corp. and Bloodaxe Books; Màrtainn Mac an t-Saoir / Martin MacIntyre, 'Tools of the Trade', by permission of the author; Somhairle MacGill-Eain / Sorley MacLean, from 'Cumha Chaluim Iain MhicGil-Eain' / 'Elegy for Calum I. MacLean', from O Choille gu Bearradh: Dain chruinnichte / from *White Leaping Flame: Collected Poems* (Carcanet / Birlinn, 2011), by permission of Carcanet; Jo McDougall, 'Mammogram' from *Satisfied with Havoc* (Autumn House Poetry, 2004), reprinted with the permission of The Permissions Company, Inc. on behalf of Autumn House Poetry, www.autumnhouse.org; Roger McGough, 'Catching Up on Sleep' from *Collected Poems* (Penguin, 2004) (Roger McGough, 2016), is printed by permission of United Agents (www.unitedagents. co.uk) on behalf of Roger McGough; Czesław Miłosz, 'Gift', from *New & Collected Poems, 1931–2001* (Allen Lane, The Penguin Press, 2001) © Czesław Miłosz Royalties Inc, 1988, 1991, 1995, 2001, reproduced by permission of Penguin Books Ltd; Edwin Morgan, 'At Eighty', from *Cathures: New Poems, 1997–2001* (Carcanet, 2002), by permission of the publisher; Chloe Morrish, 'Adam, There Are Animals', by permission of the author; Bernard O'Donoghue, 'Going Without Saying', from *Gunpowder* (Chatto, 1995), by permission of the author; John O'Donohue, 'Beannacht / Blessing', from *Echoes of Memory* (Transworld Publishing, 2010) by permission of the author's Estate; Sharon Olds,

'His Stillness', from *The Father* (Jonathan Cape, 2009), reprinted by permission of the Random House Group Ltd; Theodore Roethke, 'My Papa's Waltz', from *Collected Poems* (Faber & Faber Ltd, 1967), by permission of the publisher; Michael Rosen, 'These are the Hands' by Michael Rosen (© Michael Rosen), is printed by permission of United Agents (www.unitedagents.co.uk) on behalf of the author; Jelaluddin Rumi translated by Coleman Barks, 'The Guest House', from *Rumi: Selected Poems*, translated by Coleman Barks with John Moynce, A.J. Arberry, Reynold Nicholson (Penguin Books, 2004), by permission of Penguin Books Ltd; Karen Patricia Schofield, 'Myeloma Moths' from *The Annual Hippocrates Prize Anthology 2016*, by permission of the author; Helen Catherine Sheppard, 'Opening' from *The Annual Hippocrates Prize Anthology 2017*, by permission of the author; Andrea Wershof Schwartz, 'The First Death' from *The Annual Hippocrates Prize Anthology 2016*, by permission of the author; Iain Crichton Smith, 'The Old Lady', from *New Collected Poems* edited by Matthew McGuire (Carcanet, 2011), by permission of the publisher; John Stone, 'Talking to the Family' from *Music from Apartment 8: New and Selected Poems* Copyright © 2004 reprinted with the permission of Louisiana State University Press; Marc Straus, 'Luck' from *Not God: A Play in Verse*, Copyright © 2006 by Marc J. Straus, published 2006 by TriQuarterly Books/ Northwestern University Press, all rights reserved; Nuala

Watt, 'Eye Chart' by permission of the author; Hamish Whyte, 'The Precious 10 Minutes', by permission of the author.